THE ONLY PRAYER
I'LL EVER PRAY:

LET MY PEOPLE GO

Donald R. Wright

TO FREDDIE

HOPE YOU ENJOY THE READ. STAY
WELL AND PURSUE TRUTH!

Donald

9/11/2010

First published by Dog Ear Publishing
4010 W. 86th Street, Ste H
Indianapolis, IN 46268
www.dogearpublishing.net

ISBN: 978-160844-291-1

This book is printed on acid-free paper.

Printed in the United States of America

ACKNOWLEDGEMENTS

To my wife, thank you for everything since our lives were joined. Your support, patience and most of all your tolerance are irreplaceable. In order to make this idea a reality, I needed and received your assistance. I love you.

To my daughter, it was you that inspired me to write this book. You were really in tune with my thoughts and feelings, and you knew how important it was for me to share them with others. Thanks for the inspiration and being with me on this journey. Continue to find your truths and do not be fearful when it is time to change. You are very special. I love you too.

To my friend Joe, you are a stalwart for truth and a fearless proponent for justice and correctness. Thank you for your support and encouragement.

I extend appreciation to Norm R. Allen, Jr. for his encouragement and work with African Americans for Humanism and to Shondrah Tarrezz Nash for her comments and enthusiastic support.

FOREWORD

"And out of the ground made the Lord God to grow every tree that is pleasant to the sight, and good for food; the tree of life also in the midst of the garden, and the tree of knowledge of good and evil…And the Lord God commanded man, saying, Of every tree of the garden thou mayest freely eat: But of the tree of knowledge of good and evil, thou shalt not eat of it: for in the day that thou eatest thereof thou shalt surely die" (Gen. 2: 9, 16-17 King James Version).

The majority of my life thus far was consumed with the Christian religion. Then one day in 2002, my father ate the fruit of the tree of knowledge of good and evil, just like the serpent told Eve; my father's eyes were opened. He began to see, I mean really see, and his thirst for knowledge has never been refreshed since. It hasn't been a day that he has not read, seen, or heard something that brings light to the darkness. However, he is not alone in his quest. That day he handed me a piece of the fruit of the tree of knowledge of good and evil, I ate it, devoured it actually, and my eyes opened. Many, okay most, will say that my father forced me to see what he saw, do what he did, and feel how he felt.

However, I truly did see what he saw, wanted to do what he did, and I felt what he felt. But now here I am a few years later finally eating fruit that I pulled off the tree myself. I am seeing things in a way he didn't see. So the knowledge being shared is mutual.

To my father, this has been quite the experience being a part of your growth. I do not regret, nor resent that day in 2002. I thank you Daddy for giving me a piece of your fruit. Thank you for assisting me to open my own eyes and see the truth. You and Mommy taught me to think and seek my own way. Thank you.

To the reader, my father has revolutionary power, sincerity, but most of all truth in his words. He has decoded this Matrix we call religion. He explains his journey; so take that journey with him as you read. Have an open mind, open heart, but most of all open your eyes. It is our Human Nature to question, seek, and find. It has just been suppressed, and even taken from us to do either. So I suggest as you read, do not deny your Human Nature, but embrace your own godliness. If you know better you do better. Take a piece of this fruit, no need to be afraid of death, this fruit will give you an everlasting life of truth, and not lies. This can be your amazing grace. For we are lost, and we can be found. We are blind, but now we have the information to see. So, gain the wisdom that you naturally seek.

In Truth, Peace, and Love,

Xandelyn B. Wright
July 2009

TABLE OF CONTENTS

PREFACE

There are an estimated 15% of the population in the United States that are non-religious; atheists, agnostics, deists, secular humanists, etc. To provide some perspective, that percentage clearly outnumbers blacks and substantially outnumbers the Jews and Muslims. Their voices are seldom heard as a group. Unless my history lessons have failed, I do not recall any wars and conflicts that were started by representatives of this group. I do not recall an abortion clinic being bombed or a doctor murdered by an atheist or agnostic. I fail to recall a suicide bomber that was identified as non-religious. I am not aware of a non-religious group of people that demands ownership of land, proclaims independence while easily depending primarily on the financial support of another nation, and always on the brink of war. I may be mistaken in stating that there are no indications where the infidels douse the believers with everlasting punishment and torment for refusing to agree with their beliefs. Contrary to what most Christians think, nations with lesser religious influence experience fewer conflicts with other nations and less crime among its citizens. Denmark and Sweden are considered the least religious countries in the world, but enjoy strong economies, low crime rates, high standards of living and social equality. It is very disappointing that the crime rate among blacks in America is high considering we are the most religious race of people in the country. It is interesting that most racists (white supremacist) are very religious. The ills of the universe cannot be blamed on the non-religious.

Considering these assessments, non-religious persons may be more respectful and appreciative of human sanctity. The advent of world peace and sustaining human existence are more probable through the views and attitudes of the non-religious. However, these assessments leave others to debate the very few positives and even fewer benefits of participating in or adapting to a religion. We do not know precisely why religion exists or why it is so important in the lives of so many people, but it can be rejected. This has guided me, a black man from the south, into writing this book.

My point of focus in this book is on organized religion, primarily Christianity, not matters of altered states of consciousness and spirituality, and why I think blacks in America should strongly and urgently consider disregarding the need. This book, my first, is the result of my revised thoughts regarding religion and its practices. I was compelled to alter my thinking, then my behavior because of the acquisition of information that resonates as truth; that which stands alone. Truth is clarity. To seek the truth, acquire it, and fail to act on it is a travesty. My hope is that during your reading, you will somehow displace emotions with reasonable observation of a presentation of thoughts and some facts worthy of mere consideration. Your opportunity for change, if any, may not be painless and swift but I encourage your embracement. This book is based on a practical, common sense perspective of religion and its harmful influence. This view on religion is business of importance, for the only prayer I will ever pray is "let my people go."

Donald R. Wright
July 2009

Chapter 1:

DAWN OF ENLIGHTENMENT

"When you control a man's thinking you do not have to worry about his actions."

- Carter G. Woodson

"Many people would rather die than think; in fact most do."

- Bertrand Russell

When reading books on intimate subjects such as religion, I have always felt a need to know as much about the writer as available. While reading, I try to imagine them as if we are having a conversation. The person is the message. Their background and experiences contribute to their thoughts and attitudes. So I want to begin by sharing some details about me and how my evolution occurred.

I was born September 16, 1952 in Fayette, Alabama to Harold (father) and Willie Mack (mother) Wright. My father died in July 1989 at the age of 63 and my mother died in November 2003 at the age of 73. Each death was a result of cancer and their final moments were in the same hospital in Tuscaloosa, Alabama. Most of their adult years required battling with health issues. Even in their death, they provided something special for my life.

My parents were the best. They met the requirements and made provisions for their children according to their capabilities, as quality parents should. My father graduated from high school and regretted not attending college, while my mother lamented not receiving a high school diploma. She had to quit school to take care of her younger siblings. We learned later about how much abuse as a teenager mom had to tolerate. Too bad she did not write her story. As a result, they were committed to providing educational opportunities for their three children. Elease, the first born, and I both earned degrees from Tennessee State University, while Evalina, the middle child and the one with the higher intellect, chose not to attend college. Dad demanded high academics and participation in extra-curricula activities, especially athletics, and certainly we were required to be active in church as they were. Dad had a wonderful singing voice and sang in a gospel quartet. I can still hear his rendition of "Milky White Way." I inherited my religion, similar to most religious people, but I missed the singing voice, not to imply that all religious people can sing. In the sixties, high school sports for girls were phased out, but my sisters were skilled enough as a result of dad's coaching to compete with the boys on the playgrounds or the "thickets" where we played baseball and football. In high school, I lettered in basketball and baseball. Mom's role was to emphasize common sense, personal responsibility, and to assure our learning of the facts of life. We were taught to maintain God in our lives and to respect people in authority. Our family was very close and very supportive of one another.

My parents wedding date was five months before Elease's birth. Evalina was born two years later, and I, dad's much-anticipated son, arrived two years subsequent. According to them, that was not the perfect plan for starting a family but back then marriage was the right thing to do when pregnancy was evident. Attitudes have really changed since that era. Dad could have avoided the situation similar to many other men, but I learned my father's character to be that of always accepting responsibility plus he loved my mother.

My parents were hard workers and first responders in times of need for their families and the community. It was in their DNA to sacrifice for others. A story was constantly told about my father, that during a high school football game, he sacrificed his thigh pads for the use by a teammate who for some reason did not have his pair and was in fear of injury. As a result, dad's leg injury prevented a football scholarship and would be a lifetime ailment. Our little town, population 10,000, misses them maybe as much my sisters and I.

There are many questions associated with the event of my birth. Why this date and year? Why this town, state and country? Why to the union of these individuals? Within this amazing process of human creation, why was I fortunate to be born without any significant defects? The answers to these questions can set the course to comprehending humanity's quest of understanding a life's journey. That journey consists of birth, life, and death. Obviously, I did not have any input to the decisions leading to my birth.

On the opposite end of the journey, I am still pondering my influence on the exact moment of death, the greatest fear of most humans. I hope to delay the experience of death for at least an additional 56 years. Not out of fear, but for the ambition of acquiring more truth and then sharing it with others for their examination.

The second phase of the journey, life, is the known. At this juncture of life, I have come to know, in addition to many other truths, that the act of living is guided dominantly by our individual decisions and each step during this phase of the journey will serve as training and preparation for other decisions. Experience is a valuable teacher. Each wakened moment is utilized to navigate the tribulations and pleasures of life, achieving success, and the pursuit of happiness as defined far too often by our culture and environment. My parents, sisters, relatives, friends, neighbors, educational institutions, and religion each played a significant role in my decision-making ability a few years prior to adulthood. Some decisions may be impossible to attribute to whom or what contributed the major influence. The quality of some of those decisions may never be affirmed. I offer a message in summary that we are all teachers; the life we live is what we teach.

I graduated from college in 1975 with a degree in electrical engineering. It was not high intellect but discipline of time and study that allowed my accomplishment. I knew my purpose for being there and failure was not an option. There were plenty of job opportunities and the enforcement of affirmative action was at the forefront. The Fortune 500 Company that I chose to begin my engineering career felt the coercion. I am an example of affirmative action providing the opportunity that a qualified black man in a racist society would not otherwise receive.

The past eight years have been my dawn of enlightenment; the observance and practice of truth. My immediate family, wife and daughter, would probably describe it as the "what's next" era because of the numerous changes in rapid succession. I have made alterations to my behavior and thoughts regarding health, our monetary system, politics, and most dramatically religion. As a family, we made changes in our diet because of acquired knowledge regarding diabetes and its primary contributors. We made changes in household cleaning and personal care products because of learning about cancer and its causes. Considering how difficult change is for most people, for me, each one was painless and swift; utilizing logic, reason, and the minimum influence of emotions. I discovered that a right combination of motivation and knowledge could produce a desire to implement an immediate change in behavior.

Now that I know the truth, religious holidays no longer exist on my calendar and it is highly probable that you can contact me at the office on December 25th. It is a normal business day except quieter. However, it would have been very difficult halting Christmas celebration when our daughter was a pre-teen instead of during her sophomore year in college. No more Christmas shopping.

The decision to become a self-employed engineering consultant in January 2002 was the key that unlocked the chains that held me in mental bondage and lifted the veil that blinded me from the truth. The inspiration for that decision was in place a few months prior when I determined the sources contributing to my occupational frustration. In this escape from corporate slavery, I finally acquired ownership of my precious resource, time. I embraced the opportunity to set priorities regarding business and personal growth. I discovered an interest in areas other than engineering HVAC control systems. Fervent reading was now my window into the world. I had no idea how much truth was within my grasp. Since this is a book about religion, I will quote a religious book, "the truth will set you free." However, it takes courage to act on truth, especially when acting alone.

In 2004, I made a commitment to be a more knowledgeable Christian in lieu of being a handicapped Christian; totally dependent upon pastors, preachers, and teachers for interpretation and instruction regarding the Bible. That commitment was the result of too many disappointing church experiences. In reading this book, some may suspect me being angry at the church or religion in general, but I consider my disposition to be that of warlike disapproval of perpetual lies and deceit. Throughout my adult life following college, as an active member of the church, I was becoming more inquisitive about the Bible and developing increased awareness of inappropriate behavior by pastors and preachers. It was disturbing to hear them preaching a behavior that they did not adhere. My tolerance level for this hypocrisy had reached its lowest. Between 2003 and 2006, I had been a member of four different churches.

I enrolled in a local Bible college in January 2005 for coursework to learn how to study the Bible and develop some basic skills for teaching Christian principles. I completed three courses, one per semester, in three consecutive semesters. These courses focused on techniques not theological training. I purchased different versions of the Bible, commentaries, dictionaries, encyclopedias, a Bible atlas, and computer software Bible study programs. Only a few of these items were required for the coursework. I acquired two other significant books, *The Lost Books of the Bible* and *Lost Scriptures-Books that Did Not Make It into the New Testament*. My home library increased substantially. I had a hunger and thirst for knowledge and truth as never before. My Christian evolution had begun. This change was so apparent that some of my family and friends made comments suggesting I was being called to the ministry. I must admit that I almost agreed with their assessment because I pondered the idea that maybe it was God inspiring my clarity of interpretation. At this point I was a devout Christian.

As a result of my consistent and intense self-study, using the Internet and many books, I concluded that the Christianity as I was taught and practicing was overwhelmingly different from the Bible. Some of the principles Jesus taught are more aligned with socialism as compared to capitalism. I was able to observe that Paul's message was taught regularly and with more emphasis in comparison to the message of Jesus. I was able to grasp that Paul's rise to apostleship was through self-appointment, hunger for recognition and influence. He was the central founder of Christianity. In Acts 14:14, both Paul and Barnabas are referred to as apostles, so why did Paul's writings become the major foundation for church doctrine but the writings of Barnabas and others are ignored? I was shocked to discover that in his writings, Paul does not refer to a historical Jesus; place of birth, death, or burial, mother and father, or the specific miracles. Jesus Christ may have been a figment of Paul's imagination. It was apparent that the Gospels do not indicate Jesus encouraging the establishment and organization of a church, the appointment of pastors and leaders nor to refer to them as Reverend.

I concluded that the Gospels do not record Jesus suggesting to disavow keeping the Sabbath; the seventh day, which according to the calendar is Saturday. Studying the Gospel of John provided clarity as to the foundation of Christians' negative attitude towards Jews. Christianity was now very questionable.

The *Age of Reason* written by Thomas Paine in 1794 was the switch that illuminated my view of religions, especially Christianity. I will forever consider myself fortunate to discover this tremendous work of literature via the Internet. He wrote about the harmfulness of religions and how they prevented free thought. He provided a historical perspective on Islam and Judaism, and uncovered the fallacies of the Bible. In some of his other writings, he referenced the Council of Nicaea. The Council of Nicaea, early 4th century, played a major role in the origin of the Bible and Christianity. Thomas Paine (1737 – 1809) was an advocate for the abolition of slavery in America and was a founding member of the anti-slavery society, The Society for the Relief of Free Negroes Unlawfully Held in Bondage, formed in Philadelphia April 14, 1775. He is an American hero because his writing of the pamphlet *Common Sense* sparked the original colonies into declaring independence from Great Britain.

I was compelled to find others that presented similar ideas and more facts for my consideration. To my surprise, the amount of information was astonishing. Men such as W.E.B. DuBois, Carter G. Woodson, Robert G. Ingersoll, and Bertrand Russell have been my sources of inspiration. The result was my escape from religion in 2006. I became an infidel.

As a substitute for being a religious person, I prefer to be a quality person. There are five characteristics that make a quality person: (1) assume total responsibility for your welfare, (2) honor your commitments, (3) do not harm other people, (4) do not harm the environment, and (5) assist other people in their times of need.

During the past three years while continuing life's journey on a different path free from religion, I have personally encountered only a few blacks that share my viewpoint on organized religions. That position is to stand clear of all organized religions currently in existence in this universe due to their inability to offer truth in its totality. Religion, especially Christianity, is too harmful for the well being of humankind.

> *As in my political works my motive and object have been to give man an elevated sense of his own character, and free him from slavish and superstitious absurdity of monarchy and heredity government, so in my publications on religious subjects, my endeavors have been directed to bring man to a right use of the reason that God has given him, to impress on him the great principles of divine morality, justice, mercy, and a benevolent disposition to all men, and to all creatures, and to inspire in him a spirit of trust, confidence, and consolation in his creator, unshackled by the fables of books pretending to be the word of God.*
>
> *– Thomas Paine*

Chapter 2:

WHAT IS RELIGION?

"Is God willing to prevent evil, but not able?
Then he is not omnipotent. Is he able, but not
willing? Then he is malevolent. Is he both able
and willing? Then whence cometh evil. Is he nei-
ther able nor willing? Then why call him God?
                    - Epicurus (341 – 270 BCE),
                                Greek philosopher

There are very few human activities in our society where a religious expression or gesture is not offered. In fact, the frequency is overwhelming. After sneezing, the person in sounding distance is compelled to extend a "bless you." Expect to receive prayers from the group during a tragedy. I cannot imagine a politician ending a speech without "God Bless America." At Major League baseball games since the event of 911, God Bless America is sung during the 7th inning stretch. Athletes point and verbalize to whom should be credited for their success; scoring a touchdown, hitting a home-run, or winning the race. The meetings of non-religious organizations have on the agenda an opening prayer or invocation. Religious bumper stickers are highly visible. Stop! Look! Listen! Someone is thanking God for something this very moment. A meal without a prayer to "bless the food" endangers the flavor and nutrition. Fried chicken and peach cobbler need a lot of prayer to help prevent heart disease and diabetes. It was not until I was able to expel myself from its grips that I observed the incredible magnitude of religion.

Who or what is God? Why am I here? What is the purpose of life? Are humans more important than animals and plants? When and how was this universe created? What happens after death? These are only a few of the more puzzling questions humans have attempted to answer throughout history. History indicates as humans found answers albeit mysteriously, religion followed and became a complex human institution. Religion is a significant part in the lives of many people. How significant depends on the benefits each individual perceives as vital to survival.

The human body is an incredible machine. Who should be given credit for its creation, how and when the creation occurred is still being debated. This debate does not overshadow the amazement of the creation or evolution. At the center of this machine is the brain. The brain activates the mind. The human mind is proving to be limitless. An attribute of the mind is imagination. The conscious mind cannot distinguish between imagination and reality. Religion imposes on human behavior by influencing humans' imagination thus altering their reality. Monotheistic religions such as Judaism, Christianity, and Islam, attempt to direct humans' thoughts toward a personal God, a God that secures and sustains all beings in the entire universe. To them, this is the same God of all creation. This God decides who lives and dies, and by what means. I can imagine God hovering above the earth contemplating human death, "hmmm, who shall it be and should it be by murder, cancer, tornado, bridge collapse, plane crash, or lightening?" Christianity conditions humans to accept the reality of places called heaven and hell, and the means to attain salvation, the avoidance of hell, is through the person of Jesus Christ, God's son. Hell is much more vivid to Christians than heaven, just read the Bible's book of Revelation. The threat of hell is effectively similar to an unfriendly person holding a loaded gun to your head.

If God created humans and gave them the ability to think, reason, imagine, and make decisions, then most religions, especially Christianity, promote restriction to use these natural attributes. When a concept or idea is presented to an individual and that person uses their ability to reason and then decides to reject or disagree with that concept, a religion or institution that suggests a punishment for that decision causes a major conflict with a natural gift from God. Why would God empower you with something and punish you for using it? With this gift of mental capacity, humans would have the ability to choose, to reject or deny even the existence of God. If God is the creator, a godly person would respect all creation enough to never impose religious dogma on a fellow human. A godly person would encourage all humans to pursue truth that will suffice for the sake of the universe and its need for peace, harmony and sustainability.

The Creation Story, Sin, and Human Sacrifice

Most religions and their denominations have their holy book for guidance and definition. The holy book or books define God. Judaism has the Torah, Talmud and Tanakh. Islam has the Koran. The Christians' holy book is the Bible. According to Christians, it is the inerrant word of God regardless of the version or translation. Christianity identifies this gift, the ability to choose, through a term called free will. When studying this from the Bible's perspective, the conflict with free will is introduced in Genesis with the creation story. Approximately 6,000 years ago, God created man in his own image, using dust from the ground and his breath, man (humans), as we know it today became a living being. Archeological studies show that Aboriginal people have been in Australia for at least 40,000 years. Modern science dates the earth's age to be near 3,600 million years. Back to Genesis. The first man was named Adam. Adam's helpmate, woman, was created from Adam's rib and named Eve. We assume that the attributes of thought, reason, and imagination were given at this point because the Bible does not indicate how the human mind was activated. God gives Adam instructions regarding a tree that they should not eat its fruit. A question that Christians and other religions that adhere to this creation story are challenged to explain is "Why did God give humans the propensity of disobedience?" The story does not indicate Adam being taught anything about disobedience nor what it means to die, yet God chooses to punish Adam for using a gift that God gave him. I imagine Adam was then introduced to a new term called confusion. Eve tried to blame the snake; after all it was the most cunning of all the other animals.

It is intriguing to comprehend the concept of man being created in God's image. We could certainly benefit from a photo of Adam and Eve. This photo would give us the true image of God and we would know the color of the first human's skin tone. The author of Genesis does not attempt to describe the physical appearance of the first couple. I will conclude that the author, whomever that may be, was not interested in providing that information. Did Adam and Eve resemble men and women of today? Apparently their reproductive organs functioned to produce offspring, three sons, and the multiplication of mankind was set into motion. Without any instructions, they were able to engage sexually. According to the creation story, all humans are the result of Adam's sperm and Eve's egg.

Christians would prefer to explain the eating of the fruit as to how sin was introduced to mankind and because of Adam all humans are sinful. Some explain it by saying that this act caused humans to have a sinful nature, which means it is now natural for humans to sin or have the desire to sin. Since disobedience is a sin, and Adam had this natural ability to disobey, then this perfect God, the creator, must be okay with this attribute because he gave it to Adam. Being told by loving Christians that you are a sinner or you were born in sin cannot possibly be good for a person's self-image. What normally follows, in an attempt to restore one's self-image, is the statement that Jesus Christ died for your sins even the ones you will commit in the future, so don't worry be happy.

The word sin strikes fear in the minds of Christian believers. Sin is a direct correlation to hell, a place of everlasting torment. The concept of sin was created by Christians only to offer solutions through the Bible. This is similar to a person burglarizing your house and returning the next day to sell you a security system.

In line with this message concerning human frailty, the story of Jesus, God incarnate, gives us a depiction of a human that was sinless in his 33 man-years. Also, the story of Jesus implies that he was immune from this sin nature that all other humans inherit. Is this because of the absence of a biological father? Is the sperm of a man sinful? Is a woman born in sin also? Is the egg of a woman sinful? Would Mary be considered Jesus' biological mother? Was Mary born in sin? How could Mary give a biological birth to a sinless human being? Rational and logical answers to these questions would be significant in aiding Christianity in becoming a little more palatable. Also, it would be much appreciated if Christians would establish a definitive date of Jesus' birth and death. Christian scientists can assist in providing the world some acceptable facts. The funds certainly are available through the church to finance a project of this magnitude. Just ask the Catholic Church for the money. Today, many Christians will acknowledge the deceit of the Christmas celebration, as more are viewing it as commercialism. But I understand the challenge considering the contradictions in the Gospels regarding these events. Also, it would have been beneficial for the writers of the Gospels to provide a few details of Jesus' life between the ages 12 and 30. I find it difficult to accept that this amazing human that is credited with so many miracles had 18 years of activity unworthy of documentation. Regarding the purpose of Jesus' life, why would God transform to human existence to sacrifice himself to himself for the forgiveness of human sins? If God is as the Bible indicates, I suggest he (excuse the gender notation) could probably forgive without the need for a brutal execution and gory details. If you cannot imagine the bloody details of the crucifixion, try viewing Mel Gibson's movie "The Passion of the Christ." It grossed, no pun intended, over $370 million in the U.S. alone using graphic illustrations to make these events a lasting memory. By the way, the forgiveness of sin was introduced in the Old Testament (Ex 32:32).

A Fairy Tale and Its Unknown Writer

Another intriguing story in the Bible is the one where Jesus walks on water and then shortly, Peter accomplishes the same feat. This story is recorded in Matthew Chapter 14, Mark Chapter 6, and John Chapter 6. But only in Matthew is the story told of Peter's miraculous walk. To refrain from being too critical, it is fascinating to observe the differences in how these authors describe this same event. Peter's ability to transcend nature is suddenly disabled due to his fear of the wind and losing faith.

> *Matthew 14:(28) Peter said to Him, "Lord, if it is You, command me to come to You on the water." (29) And He said, "Come!" And Peter got out of the boat, and walked on the water and came toward Jesus. (30) But seeing the wind, he became frightened, and beginning to sink, he cried out, "Lord, save me!" (31) Immediately Jesus stretched out His hand and took hold of him and said to him, "You of little faith, why did you doubt?"*
>
> *- New American Standard Bible*

According to the story in at least one account, there were other persons there to witness two humans walking on water and not any of their testimonies are documented. I am very curious to know why Mark and John did not record Peter's miracle. If I am not mistaken, John, the most loved disciple per John's own description, should have been there. But I am more amazed that Peter doesn't write about this in his two epistles (1 Peter and 2 Peter) included in the Bible. The opportunity is available in terms of subject matter because in 1 Peter Chapter 1 he talks about faith. How could he dismiss the opportunity to describe his feelings achieving something this incredible? Maybe, Peter did not write these documents. Maybe the event wasn't important enough. Maybe the event didn't happen. This story makes another great fairy tale similar to flying reindeers. Where did the authors of Matthew, Mark and John get their information? For an example, Matthew 9:9 reads as if it was written by someone other than Matthew.

> *Matthew 9:9 As Jesus went on from there, He saw a man called Matthew, sitting in the tax collector's booth; and He said to him, "Follow Me!" And he got up and followed Him.*
> *- New American Standard Bible*

Each book of the Bible should be examined from the perspective of proof of authorship.

Mis-education of Christians

Most intellectuals define Christianity as a religion. Among most Christians, there is disconnect in their view of Christianity as such. Through the effort of well-trained preachers and teachers over many years using a consistent message, it is undeniably accepted as a way of life rather than a religion. In today's tenet, some theologians define it as relational in comparison to that old time religion. To others, being religious is synonymous to fanaticism. Christianity does not require as much in terms of behavior, compared to other religions, such as keeping the Sabbath, not eating pork, or praying a certain number of times per day. The only requirement is to accept Jesus Christ as your lord and savior. Accept this as truth and you will avoid eternal fire in the mist of hell regardless of how many people you hurt. You will be forgiven. There are five Fundamentals of Christianity: (1) inerrancy of the Bible, (2) virgin birth and the deity of Jesus, (3) atonement by God's grace and having faith, (4) bodily resurrection of Jesus, and (5) authenticity of Jesus' miracles. I had been a practicing Christian for over fifty years including birth into a Christian family and a former deacon in a Baptist church. That allows me some knowledge through study and experiences. Some of those experiences were grave and heightened my awareness of fallacies. It is easy to become and stay a Christian, which makes Christianity very attractive.

Prior to 2006, I had not given considerable thought and interest to a religion other than Christianity. It was not encouraged by my parents or the churches I had attended, to extend the effort to study other religions, particularly Judaism and Islam. I had been conditioned to believe that Christianity was the only true way to God. It has been a joy of discovery to invest the time to study other religions. For the sake of religions, we have the weekend; Friday for Muslims, Saturday for Jews and some Christians, and Sunday for most Christians. This study allowed me to compare many of the world's religions and their vast denominations, and easily conclude that the best religion for me would be no religion.

My journey away from Christianity began when I made the commitment to study the Bible in the same scholarly manner used in studying my engineering books. I was finally anxious to know what this so called "holy book" was about, including the origin. It did not take long to note the contradictions, vagueness, and how logical questions remained unanswered. As significant as Christians want us to think of it, the Bible is very limited in addition to the many contradictions (a few are listed at the end of this book). A contradiction is a stumbling block to truth. Discarding the need for thorough study of the Bible and lacking the desire to ask probing questions are the primary contributors to the mis-education of Christians. Compare the attendance at so called Bible study services and Sunday school to worship services. This mis-education prevents most Christians from providing reasonable debate in support of their belief system because of their lack of knowledge.

The Bible ranks low in my literary evaluation while it does provide some historical value and a few suggestions of principles to live by, but adhering to the demand of Christians of its divinity, infallibility, and being inspired by God is irrational and therefore unacceptable. Their entire belief system and doctrine regarding the Bible is based on Paul's writing of

2 Timothy 3:16-17:

> *All scripture is inspired by God and profitable for teaching, for reproof, for correction for training in righteousness; so that the man of God may be adequate, equipped for every work.*
> *- New American Standard Bible*

Paul could not have been referring to the current Bible because it did not exist during the time of this letter to Timothy. The word scripture most likely was referencing the Old Testament or the Hebrew writings used by the Jews. That means Christianity and Judaism should be almost identical in practice including the observance of "holy days". The truth can be painful. It is comical to watch politicians during their taking of the oath of office place their hand on the Bible to assure their integrity so help them God and within 24 hours they make false promises for the sake of campaign funding for the next election. The Bible can't help these people.

The Proof of God is in Doubt

Today, my only perception of God (word is used only due to a lack of a substitute) is through nature and the existence of so many amazing things in their natural order, not through a religion. The amazing plants and animals and their many species, the moon, and the night sky filled with stars, are examples of what comprise this incredible universe. As an engineer, I am a practitioner of science with a responsibility to offer recommendations and conclusions based on facts and principles. Meteorologists can provide accurate weather forecast and hurricane tracking. In 2007, scientists announced 700 new species of organisms discovered down in the Weddell Sea of Antarctica. Science has provided explanations for many natural occurrences but major questions still remain unanswered. For example, how was the sun created and will it exist forever? Due to a lack of a rational explanation, other than assigning the creation of the sun and its daily disappearance to God, I cannot begin to prove that there is a God. Is there a human that can? This God that I assign as the creator of the sun and how it produces the seasons, is this the God that instructed a father (Abraham) to kill his son (Isaac) to prove faith? Is this the same God that spoke to Moses and Muhammad, and had spiritual sex with a virgin that gave birth to a son called Jesus? Is this the same God that is jealous, demands worship and money offerings? Is this the same God that created this magnificent universe and plans to destroy it in the very near future? I seriously doubt it. The God of the Old Testament punished the children of Israel many times for worshipping other Gods. I am fascinated that this omnipotent creator as written in the Bible could experience the emotion of jealousy. It is extremely mystical.

The sun is vital to our existence. Who or what sustains this permanent source of both life-giving and life-taking energy? Humans truly understand the significance of the sun and early civilizations thought it to be deserving of worship. The practice of sun worshipping is the foundation that became the origin of symbols for many mythologies. Christianity's symbol of Jesus as the "son of God" appears to be a representation of the sun from God the creator of the entire universe. The study of ancient African religions and spirituality, this includes Egypt, reveals an origin that Christianity may be assimilating. One of the many Egyptian Gods, Horus, pre-dates Christianity and Jesus by thousands of years. Horus was born of a virgin Isis on December 25th, died and was resurrected after three days. He too was labeled as God incarnate.

In line with Horus, the worshiping of Mithra, a sun God of ancient Persia, preceded Christianity by approximately 600 years. Mithra had similarities with Jesus. He was born on December 25th, a teacher that traveled with 12 companions, and referred to as the good shepherd, the way, the truth and the light, the redeemer, savior, and messiah. There were ceremonies that included baptism to remove sins, and a sacred meal of bread and wine. The holy day for this sun God was Sunday. His father was the creator God, Ahura-Mazda.

It is very easy to conclude that the story of Jesus was influenced by other mystical godly figures. Christians celebrating Jesus' birth on December 25th is a hoax, especially since the Bible fails to provide a definitive date. Adoration for the sun, establishing a central figure for worship, and providing a book to support the controlling institution, does not prove the existence of God the creator. Rational thinking and factual evidence should be our guide, not mysticism, beliefs, and blind faith.

Religion Defined

A family living in Adamsville, Texas had started to experience strange sounds and items becoming misplaced. They decided to hire a professional to provide explanations and solutions. The professional identified the source to be a closet that contains an unfriendly spirit. The professional convinced the family that to negate the affects of this spirit, the door to this closet must never be open. They are safe and secure as long as that door remains closed.

This story is completely fictional, but represents an analogy of most religions, especially Christianity. You are safe, secure, and entitle to everlasting life as long as you don't open your mind to question the Bible's origin and its contents. To be a Christian, it is not necessary to know the parents of Cain's wife and who was guiding the society in which she lived. To be a Christian, it is not necessary to know how many nations existed when God decided to drown all living organisms except a select few. It would be foolish for a Christian to inquire about the means by which the Egyptians, according to Genesis Chapter 41, sold grain to the people of all the earth. To be a Christian, it is not beneficial to know if Matthew heard directly from Joseph about his dream regarding Jesus' birth. Opening your mind may allow credulity to escape. The people that thrive on your membership, that constitutes monetary donations, cannot afford for you to be inquisitive. Blind faith is a must.

Religion is a system by which humans devise answers to unanswerable questions and use that system to control and manipulate the thoughts and actions of other humans. In a speech delivered before the American Free Religious Association, in Boston, June 2, 1899, Robert G. Ingersoll states:

> *"In view of these facts, what, after all, is religion? It is fear. Fear builds the altar and offers the sacrifice. Fear erects the cathedral and bows the head of man in worship. Fear bends the knees and utters the prayer. Fear pretends to*

love. Religion teaches the slave-virtues; obedience, humility, self-denial, forgiveness, non-resistance. Lips, religious and fearful, tremblingly repeat this passage: "Though he slay me, yet I will trust him." This is the abyss of degradation. Religion does not teach self-reliance, independence, manliness, courage, self-defense. Religion makes God a master and man his serf. The master cannot be great enough to make slavery sweet."

Religion causes mental bondage. Any type of bondage is abusive. There is no reason, intellectually or morally, that can make any organized religion beneficial. If you deem religion to be of value to your existence, keep it personal and private. You should not require other people's acceptance for validation and surely not from coercion through threats of eternal fire and torment. A personal God is just that, personal. A rational thinking person is challenged to find any contribution to civilization by religion.

Chapter 3:

LET MY PEOPLE GO

"As my ancestors are free from slavery, I am free from the slavery of religion."
                                                    - Butterfly McQueen

It would be unacceptable to examine any topic relating to the history of blacks in the United States without including slavery. It would be an oversight to describe slavery without including the influence of religion. Religion, specifically Christianity, was used as a drug to make slaves submissive, obedient, and uninquisitive. It made this horrible institution worse.

This country was built on the backs of African slaves, my ancestors, and its history will forever be marred by this horrendous institution primarily due to the nation's inability to assist the children of slaves in coping with the trauma. The idea of expressing forgiveness will not transcend the act of transforming chattel slavery into merely a more sophisticated form of contemporary slavery. White people in America prefer not to discuss this part of their history and they are quick to state that they are not like their ancestors so let us move on. Joy Degruy Leary in her book *Post Traumatic Slave Syndrome* writes:

> *"My response to them is that I am not a slave now, nor have I ever been a slave, and as far as I know, nobody I have known personally was a slave. However, 246 years of protracted slavery guaranteed the prosperity and privilege of the south's white progeny while correspondingly relegating its black progeny to a legacy of debt and suffering. It doesn't really matter today if either of us, black or white, directly experienced or participated in slavery. What does matter is African Americans have experienced a legacy of trauma."*

America allowed its treatment of its own black citizens to permeate throughout the world and because of America's influence, other nations accepted the negative images of blacks in America as truth. I hope to someday understand the true reasons why whites developed an immense hatred for blacks. It is practically impossible to recover from a trauma when conditions associated with the cause still exist. Slavery of a people today is difficult to recognize but it surely exists in many forms. The world has failed to see or accept how the conditioning of slavery impacted our culture and transcends through family generations. Without slavery and racism, what kind of man would my father have been? What about his father?

It would be remiss in not presenting that slavery was utilized as a business plan that was very suitable for a capitalistic system. Slavery, human capital, allowed the agricultural southern states to become wealthy and powerful, and the United States to gain its foothold for becoming a world superpower.

Capitalism is dominant and thrives throughout the world. Blacks in America, regardless of our historical perspective, have learned to appreciate and promote this system. We have become as prolific in the pursuit of wealth as whites. Can you imagine Oprah Winfrey, Michael Jordan, or Jay-Z rejecting capitalism? Plantation owners needed workers, preferably cheap. The concept of slave labor made sense economically. However, capitalism promotes some disturbing side effects; greed, corruption, scarcity, and worker abuse. Some business owners of all races practice forms of slavery under the authority of capitalism by paying low wages and resenting a minimum wage law. Corporate CEO's in the United States, on the average, make 400 times the income of the lowest paid worker. W.E.B. DuBois (1868 – 1963), a great American thinker, whom I consider a pioneer for the contemporary civil rights movement, whose thoughts and ideas are seldom discussed among black Americans, wrote in his final of three autobiographies concerning capitalism and the United States:

> *"After earnest observation I now believe that private ownership of capital and free enterprise are leading the world to disaster...There was a day when the world rightly called Americans honest even if crude; earning their living by hard*

work; telling the truth no matter whom it hurt;
and going to war only in what they believed a
just cause after nothing else seemed possible.
Today we are lying, stealing, and killing. We call
all this by finer names: Advertising, Free Enter-
prise, and National Defense. But names in the
end deceive no one; today we use science to help
us deceive our fellows; we take wealth that we
never earned and we are devoting all our ener-
gies to kill, maim and drive insane, men, women,
and children who dare refuse to do what we want
done. No nation threatens us. We threaten the
world."

Slavery comes to America

It began back in 1619 when the first Africans were brought to the English colony of Jamestown, Virginia. From 1790 to 1860, the slave population grew from 500,000 to 4 million. How many Africans that survived the voyage suffered Post Traumatic Stress Disorder? How many Africans voluntarily chose death over slavery? How many blacks in America died as a result of slavery and racial hatred? How could humans treat other humans so harshly and equate them with livestock? To enlighten our perspectives, much has been written about the institution of slavery in America. The best way to incite our imagination is through the words of a former slave, Fredrick Douglas (1818-1895). He became a free man on September 3, 1838 by using a plan for escape he designed. He was separated from his mother, Harriet Bailey, as an infant. It was suspected that his father was his mother's white master. Mr. Douglas was self-educated, dedicated to the abolishment of slavery, a great orator, and describes his life in slavery in his book *Narrative of the Life of Frederick Douglas*. He describes how he suffered from hunger and the winter cold:

> *"I was kept almost naked – no shoes, no stockings, no jacket, no trousers, nothing on but a coarse tow linen shirt, reaching only to my knees. I had no bed. I must have perished with cold, but that, the coldest nights, I used to steal a bag, which was used for carrying corn to the mill. I would crawl into this bag, and there sleep on the cold, damp, clay floor, with my head in and feet out. My feet have been so cracked with the frost, that the pen with which I am writing be laid in the gashes."*

In regards to the attitude and response when a slave was killed by a slave master or an overseer he writes:

> *"It was a common saying, even among little white boys, that it was worth a half-cent to kill a nigger, and a half-cent to bury one."*

He gives us clarity as to his motivation to learn how to read:

> *"Very soon after I went to live with Mr. and Mrs. Auld, she very kindly commenced to teach me the A, B, C. After I had learned this, she assisted me in learning to spell words of three or four letters.*

Just at this point of my progress, Mr. Auld found out what was going on, and at once forbade Mrs. Auld to instruct me further, telling her, among other things, that it was unlawful, as well as unsafe, to teach a slave to read. To use his own words, further, he said, 'If you give a nigger an inch, he will take an ell. A nigger should know nothing but to obey his master—to do as he is told to do. Learning would spoil the best nigger in the world. Now, said he, 'if you teach that nigger (speaking of myself) how to read, there would be no keeping him. It would forever unfit him to be a slave. He would at once become unmanageable, and of no value to his master. As to himself, it could do him no good, but a great deal of harm. It would make him discontented and unhappy.' These words sank deep into my heart, stirred up sentiments within that lay slumbering, and called into existence an entirely new train of thought. It was a new and special revelation, explaining dark and mysterious things, with which my youthful understanding had struggled, but struggled in vain. I now understood what had been a most perplexing difficulty—to wit, the white man's power to enslave the black man. It was a grand achievement, and I prized it highly. From that moment, I understood the pathway from slavery to freedom. It was just what I wanted, and I got it at a time when I the least expected it. Whilst I was saddened by the thought of losing the aid of my kind mistress, I was gladdened by the invaluable instruction which, by the merest accident, I had gained from my master. Though conscious of the difficulty of learning without a teacher, I set out with high hope, and a fixed purpose, at whatever cost of trouble, to learn how to read."

Mr. Douglas was able to discern the hypocrisy on display within the practice of religion by some of the slave masters:

"Another advantage I gained in my new master was, he made no pretensions to, or professions of, religion; and this, in my opinion, was truly a great advantage. I assert most unhesitatingly, that the religion of the south is a mere covering for the most horrid crimes, — a justifier of the most appalling barbarity, — a sanctifier of the most hateful frauds, — and a dark shelter under, which the darkest, foulest, grossest, and most infernal deeds of slaveholders find the strongest protection. Were I to be again reduced to the chains of slavery, next to that enslavement, I should regard being the slave of a religious master the greatest calamity that could befall me. For of all slaveholders with whom I have ever met, religious slaveholders are the worst. I have ever found them the meanest and basest, the most cruel and cowardly, of all others. It was my unhappy lot not only to belong to a religious slaveholder, but to live in a community of such religionists."

During his starched position and leadership in the battle against slavery, Frederick Douglas moved from a God-centered, passive religion toward humanism and free thought.

After 246 years of forced labor, physical abuse, and psychological derailment, the abolishment of slavery and the Emancipation Proclamation did not occur too soon. The abolishment of slavery was the result of human efforts; sacrifice and commitment to the truth of freedom for all people. It was not due to a mystical miracle.

Worthy Apology

There were attempts made by some citizens and the government to remedy the wrong done to blacks in America. In 1875, a Civil Rights Act was passed stating, "all persons within the jurisdiction of the United States shall be entitled to the full and equal enjoyment of the accommodations, advantages, facilities, and privileges of inns, public conveyances on land or water, theaters, and other places of public amusement; subject only to the conditions and limitations established by law, and applicable alike to citizens of every race and color, regardless of any previous condition of servitude." In 1883 it was declared unconstitutional by the U.S. Supreme Court. The abolishment of slavery was accomplished through the efforts of both blacks and whites. The protest of slavery first occurred in 1688 by the Members of the Society of Friends (Quakers) in Germantown, Pennsylvania. Vermont was the first state to abolish it back in 1777. The last was Mississippi in 1995, only 130 years after the 13th Amendment to the Constitution. Robert G. Ingersoll (1833-1899), civil war veteran, Illinois Attorney General, abolitionist, freethinker, and a great orator, in a speech to Negroes in Galesburg, Illinois in 1867 was very apologetic:

> *"You are now citizens of many of the states, and in time you will be of all. I am astonished when I think how long it took to abolish slavery in this country. I am also astonished to think that a few years ago magnificent steamers went down the Mississippi freighted with your fathers, mothers, brothers, and sisters, and maybe some of you, bound like criminals, separated from wives, from husbands, every human feeling laughed at and outraged, sold like beasts, carried away from homes to work for another, receiving for pay only the marks of the lash upon the naked bark. I am astonished at these things. I hate to think that all this was done under the Constitution of the United States, under the flag of my country, under the wings of the eagle.*
>
> *I wonder that you- the black people- have forgotten all this. I wonder that you ask a white man to address you on this occasion, when the history of your connection with the white race is written in blood and tears—is still upon your flesh, put there by the branding-iron and the lash.*
>
> *I feel like asking your forgiveness for the wrongs that my race has inflicted upon yours. If, in the future, the wheel of fortune should take a turn, and you should in any country have white men in your power, I pray you not to execute the villainy we have taught you.*

> *One word in conclusion. You have your*
> *liberty—use it to benefit your race. Educate*
> *yourselves, educate your children, send teachers*
> *to the south. Let your brethren there be edu-*
> *cated. Let them know something of art and sci-*
> *ence. Improve yourselves, stand-by each other,*
> *and above all be in favor of liberty the world*
> *over."*

I wonder if President Obama embraces the ideals of this Illinois' statesman? Hopefully he has shared this man's biography with his children even if he chooses not to discuss it in public.

Converting the Slaves

An institution by definition with respect to sociology is an organized pattern of group behavior established and generally accepted as a fundamental part of culture. Most of today's religions meet this fundamental definition. During slavery, white slave owners systematically stripped African slaves of their spiritual and religious practices, in turn introducing and converting them to Christianity. In 1660, Charles II of England urged the Council of Foreign Plantations to convert the slaves to Christianity. This was a few years after the publishing of the King James authorized translation of the Bible in 1611. The council ordered that a letter be sent to the authorities in Barbados and Virginia commanding them to encourage the introduction of ministers who would specialize in the work of converting the newly imported Negroes to Christianity. In 1701 under William III and the Church of

England, the Society for the Propagation of the Gospel in Foreign Parts was incorporated and its mission statement included: (1) care and instruction of our people settled in the colonies, (2) the conversion of the Indian savages, and (3) the conversion of the Negroes. The concept of converting the Negroes was strongly debated. The winning side promoted the idea that if they were not converted to Christianity, they would be more readily to protest against their enslavement. Also, it was inferred that the religion practice by the Africans was savagery and blasphemous. From this inference, the concept of white people naturally having superiority over blacks, even in religion, was set in motion.

To indoctrinate the slaves with Christianity, the services were led by white Protestant evangelical preachers that taught Bible stories that justified slavery. In Leviticus 25:44-46, God grants permission to own slaves. Paul, the self-made apostle, makes it very clear in Ephesians 6:5 and 1Timothy 6:1-4 as to the attitudes slaves should have toward their masters. They also shared the idea that loyal and hard-working slaves would be rewarded in the afterlife. The introduction of spending eternity with Jesus in heaven may have persuaded the slaves that fighting for their liberty was not worth the effort in comparison. Christianity taught slaves that it was virtuous to adhere to the principles of Jesus; peaceful, passive, non-violent, and forgiving. I am reminded of these two church songs, *God Will Make a Way* and *When We All Get to Heaven*. I am unable to find any place in the New Testament where Jesus admonishes slavery. Any comment by him would have been beneficial. The Bible can be used literally to justify a vast number of inhumane activities. Adolf Hitler, a Christian, used his knowledge of the Bible and the teachings of

Martin Luther as rationale for instigating the Jewish Holocaust, another crime against humanity. Imagine having no other books to learn from, only the Bible, and the threat of severe punishment for attempting to learn how to read. Do you think those slaves were given the opportunity to ask questions during Bible study? Slaves were not to question anything. It was in their best interest to be obedient.

It was a well thought-out plan to use religion to control the slaves. In the book *African American Religious Thought: An Anthology* a reference is made to another document used by the slave masters called the *Cotton Plantation Record and Account*. It included an instruction by Thomas Affleck to the overseer:

> *"You will find that an hour devoted every Sabbath morning to their moral and religious instruction would prove a great aid to you in bringing about a better state of things amongst the Negroes. It has been thoroughly tried, and with the most satisfactory results, in many parts of the South. As a matter of mere interest it has proved to be advisable, to say nothing of it as a point of duty. The effect upon their general good behavior, their cleanliness and good conduct on the Sabbath is such as alone to recommend it to the Planter and Overseer."*

The idea of slaves finding happiness, contentment, and a better state of things through Christianity is repulsive.

The indoctrination occurred rather quickly. By the mid-eighteenth century, black preachers were ministering to free and enslaved blacks. It would be significant to know how these men were selected as preachers and what were the qualifications. Small, independent, black congregations begin to emerge in the south. It was suspected that the first recorded black congregation, it happened to be Baptist, was organized on the plantation of William Byurd in Mecklenburg, Virginia in 1758. In 1784 Richard Allen and Absalom Jones are the first black men granted licenses to preach. They established the Free African Society in Philadelphia in 1786. Andrew Bryan, in 1788, is ordained as a Baptist minister and became the minister of the First African Baptist Church of Savannah (Georgia). He gained his freedom from slavery when his master died. Two hundred and twenty one years later the black church has taken religion and Christianity to a higher level of practice. The preaching, praying, and singing can stir the emotions enough for rocks to cry out.

Religious Loyalty

For over 300 years, black people in the United States have been treated inhumanely through slavery, black codes, Jim Crow, and racism, but still maintain tremendous hope primarily through religion. To state a common phrase, black people in the United States are the most religious of all the racial groups. I chose not to use the term African American because history reveals that true African religions have no resemblance to the Christian religion currently practiced in the United States. The phrase implies that the vast majority of blacks are more apt to openly express religious connotations with firmness and vigor. Most people that practice it find emotional strength in religion, especially among blacks.

Blacks who continue the custom justify the total commitment to Christianity because the harsh condition of slavery was finally abolished due to their ancestor's prayers, belief in God and Jesus Christ, without omitting Abraham Lincoln. Without God where would we be? Without Abraham Lincoln where would we be? Blacks in America may reconsider their opinion of Abraham Lincoln if they knew his true attitude concerning Negroes. Here is what he said in his fourth debate with Stephen A. Douglas in 1858,

> *"I will say, then, that I am not, nor ever have been, in favor of bringing about in any way the social and political equality of the white and black races; that I am not, nor ever have been, in favor of making voters or jurors of Negroes, nor of qualifying them to hold office, nor to intermarry with white people; and I will say, in addition to this, that there is a physical difference between the white and black races which I believe will forever forbid the two races living together on terms of social and political equality. And in as much as they cannot so live, while they do remain together there must be the position of superior and inferior, and I as much as any other man am in favor of having the superior position assigned to the white race."*

I know this reference deviates from the subject of religion, but this statement begs us to develop a means to accurately gauge the intentions of a politician because we obviously failed in recognizing the religious intentions of the slaveholders.

It is common among many scholars, and I agree, that the black churches have been the major institution in the black communities and the only stable institution to remain from slavery. The black community views the church as powerful influence. However, I must add that being stable and influential does not mean good and without deceit. During slavery the churches allowed freedom of expression and the outpouring of emotions in their prayers, songs, and rhythmic, extemporaneous preaching style. This became the tradition followed by most black churches.

Black churches have always attempted to be a safe-haven for black people. A black church service produces transformations. It transforms mystery into reality, " what a friend we have in Jesus," and simultaneously transforms reality into non-existence. For a couple of hours black people can forget their misery; lay those burdens down. The Barna Group, a private research and resource firm, completed a survey in 2004 that examined eight elements of religious behavior and discovered that blacks were at the high end of religious activity such as reading the Bible, praying to God, giving money to churches, and watching Christian television. Blacks were also notably less likely than others to be un-churched. According to a survey in 2006 by the Barna Group, 52% of blacks are most likely to have attended a religious service in the past week. It is not difficult to find a church in the black community. In most urban areas storefront churches are common and many are next door to each other. Within three miles of my home, at this particular intersection of two major streets, there are three churches in view.

Summary and a Sincere Plea

If ten blacks are randomly selected anywhere in the country and asked the question "Are you a Christian?" I submit seven will answer yes. Why would blacks in this country adopt and promote a religion that was used as justification to enslave them? Religion, especially Christianity, promotes motivated cognition; thinking or beliefs that are based on factors other than pure reason or logic. The slave owners did not approve of slaves learning to read but supported them in practicing their Christian religion. In the transition from slavery to freedom, it appeared that an entire race of people were forced to adjust to a way of life without any possessions other than their perceived ownership of the Christian religion while being treated as subhuman. As a result, Christianity is a dominant religion among black people in America. It appears as though blacks are addicted to religion. The identification with the plight of the Hebrews enslaved by the Egyptians is the American Black religious mantra because God will deliver us from bondage too. When will God send Moses? I hope Black Americans do not continue to think that God placed our ancestors on those ships to teach them humility and unquestionable trust. Furthermore, I have not been able to find supporting documentation that confirms that the nation of Egypt held a nation of people, descendents of Jacob (Israel), in slavery for over 400 years. Frederick Douglas wrote:

> *"I have found that, to make a contented slave, it is necessary to make a thoughtless one. It is necessary to darken his moral and mental vision, and, as far as possible, to annihilate the power of reason."*

Christianity and all of its fairy tales made this horrible institution of slavery worse and continue to encourage people to diminish their desire to think. The trauma of slavery and religion, this is my plea, let my people go.

Chapter 4:

THE POOR YOU WILL HAVE

*" The proper guidance during the life of a man
should be the weight that he puts upon ethics
and the amount of consideration that he has for
others. Education has a great role to play in this
respect. Religion should have nothing to do with
a fear of living or a fear of death, but should
instead be a striving after rational knowledge."*
- Albert Einstein

In the past and present, blacks rely substantially on
the black churches and the religious leaders, and more often
than not, they have misguided the people. The leaders have
continued this pattern from slavery of presenting the church
as the only true means to solving society's problems. Look to
the church from whence cometh thou help. The best example
is the civil rights movement that occurred in the period of
1952 to 1968. The black church was the gathering place and

center of community life. The meetings to organize the Montgomery Bus Boycott were held in churches. The majority of blacks in America give total credit to the church for the success of this movement. As a result, some church leaders became very prominent; Rev. Martin Luther King, Jr., Rev. Fred Shuttlesworth, Rev. John Duffy, Rev. C.K. Steele, and Rev. Ralph Abernathy. The media's spotlight currently shines on black preachers such as Jessie Jackson, Al Sharpton, and T.D. Jakes seeking their astute opinions on social and political issues. It is ironic that Barack Obama's former pastor, Jeremiah Wright (no relation), according to the media, almost derailed Obama's campaign by expressing his opinion about our government. Now that we have a black president, his opinion may be the only one required from black people.

Business Men in the Pulpit Pursuing Wealth

In most black churches the pastor is the church, and we cannot dismiss the regularity of their failures. Christian leaders, pastors or preachers, are overwhelmed with hypocrisy and their training limits the acquisition of truth. The books that they choose to teach or preach from using their description as "God's Word" are too contaminated by man's selfish viewpoints to qualify as life's operating procedures. Their doctrines vary with the individuals that pronounce them. But in their human desire for material things, power, honor, and glorification, they expect the followers or members to submit their monetary offerings without a significant need for accountability. In other words, give your tithes and offerings freely, then let God direct the pastor in determining their use. More importantly, pastors expect the members to check their minds at the door in order for them to acquiesce whatever message they choose to preach. The result is an increase in bigger and better buildings and wealth of the leaders.

Religion in America is free enterprise and capitalism at its best. Some businesses flourish by providing their products and services to churches. The best example is the construction industry. It is obvious that religious institutions invest a lot of their congregants' hard earned dollars in buildings. It is a fascinating experience as an engineer to work with a pastor during a church construction project. Their position of authority is displayed proudly. The completion places the pastor's name in monument.

The black church is an example of how wealth is created. The pastor and his family soon can move to a larger house and drive a much nicer car. Love offerings, anniversary and birthday gifts can quickly change a personal financial statement. Regarding financial compensation for the pastor and church staff, what should be the source to determine the guidelines, the Bible or the National Association of Church Business Administration? If the Bible, then whose message is sufficient, Jesus or Paul? Most Christians choose the latter.

The primary reason for becoming a church pastor, excluding Catholic priests, is income potential. I know most of them will not admit this. Let's examine the revenue and payroll (pastor, staff, office assistants, musicians, etc.) potential of a 2000 member church.

ESTIMATED REVENUE/PAYROLL
OF A 2,000 MEMBER CHURCH

DESCRIPTION	FACTORS	PROJECTIONS
A. Number of Members	2,000	
B. Estimated Number of Working Adults (A x 50%)		1,000
C. Estimated Average Yearly Income Per Working Adult	$30,000	
D. Tithes & Offerings (C x 10%)		$3,000
E. Annual Revenue (B x D)		$3,000,000
F. Payroll Average % Church Budget	42% *	
G. Projected Annual Payroll (E x F)		$1,260,000

*Source: Christianity Today.com

How much of this $1.26 million will be allocated for the pastor? According to an article posted on the website christianpost.com Tuesday, August 19, 2008, the average senior pastor in the U.S. makes more than $80,000 a year according to a national survey. Pastors who hold a higher academic degree are paid up to $30,000 more per year than pastors without any post-secondary education.

A good suggestion may be, when a black man can't find a job he should become a preacher. A resume is not required. You only need the courage to tell people that God called.

Professional Deceivers

There is an expression amongst blacks that preachers are tight with God. Courage and sacrifice in leading the fight against racial oppression were not the essence of Martin Luther King, Jr. receiving a hero status. They must be coupled with him being a preacher. It is astounding how pastors and preachers in the black community are revered, and given a high stature, entitlements, the mantel of leadership, and the only qualification is their acknowledgment of a calling from God. Should we require them to prove the existence of God? Would it be beneficial to request proof that, without a shadow of doubt, this call was a message from God? Was the call in a deep baritone like James Earl Jones' voice? Could it have been just a dream fabricated into reality? Within a short period following this announcement, they are preaching and given authority in the lives of many people strictly on blind faith. That equates to multitudes of innocent people flocking to hear sermons that they hope will have a positive influence on their lives. It is meaningful to have the preacher to offer a prayer during an illness or a special occasion, or to act as the leader during a civil dispute because of their divine inspiration. Incredibly, they are given the opportunity to counsel on many areas of human activity assuming that the "holy spirit" will instruct them on what to say. Notwithstanding the disappointment when one of God's chosen spoke persons is found guilty of adultery, homosexuality, child molestation, rape, extortion, or theft. When this type of situation occurs, the church and the community are devastated. However, preachers do not fret very long because Christians are taught to forgive as often as seventy times seven. Please keep in mind that they are very selective as to when and to whom this forgiveness is offered.

The primary reason I terminated membership in four out of the seven churches I had joined in the past was the unveiling of the pastor's hypocrisy. While displaying a happy heterosexual marriage, one had been involved in a homosexual relationship that became a scandal that found its way into the local and national media. The church voted and by a small margin, the majority of the members in attendance at the special meeting preferred him to remain as pastor with the condition that he would agree to counseling. Our family was not alone in leaving, as a substantial number of members immediately chose to find another church. This situation was very disturbing because within two years the church membership decreased well over 50%. Homosexuality is a major theological challenge for many Christians. This incident that occurred in October 2003 was a defining moment that lead to my eventual escape from Christianity and religion.

When it comes to deception, these self-anointed individuals claiming to be called by God are professionals. The individuals with the best skills in the ability to deceive can demand higher financial compensation and more prestige.

Remaining Poor Through the Guilt of Giving

I have heard this many times, that when America gets a cold, black Americans get the flu. Our overall condition may have worsened. According to the Bible, when Jesus made the statement, "the poor you will have with you always" must have been his depiction of black people. Other than the NBA, NFL, and the prison system, blacks in America (13% in population) rank at the lowest in most areas particularly financially. In every conceivable measurement of wealth and assets, blacks own far less than whites. According to the U.S. Census Bureau, the median household income for blacks in 2006 was $32,000, and 24.3 percent of blacks were below the poverty level. Blacks remain amongst the highest in unemployment. The economic status of blacks today is pale in comparison to the "Golden Years of Black Capitalism" between 1919 and 1929 when black owned businesses were thriving.

Blacks in America would be in better financial conditions without the contrived obligation to give money to God for the support of his ministry or "Kingdom Building." Another guilt placed on the congregants is the concept of giving back to God. In my small town, we were taught to give without expecting something in return. Should that apply to God? Why does God need anything from us to achieve his purpose? According to the three Abrahamic religions, Judaism, Christianity, and Islam, God created everything without any help from us humans. Regularly, black families, barely making ends meet, are guilt ridden to give in the offering when the preacher stands there in his king-like position, designer suit, and glittering jewelry questioning, "Will a man rob God?" Imagine an elderly couple that requires expensive medications for ailments being obligated to give ten percent of their social security income to the church. Consider a family devastated from a hurricane and living on public assistance feeling compelled to deposit funds in the offering basket. There are people that give in the offering on Sunday then borrow money for lunch on Monday. It would be wise to withhold those monetary offerings in order to use them for elimination of debt and to establish funds to handle unexpected expenses that will reduce the use of credit cards. This is a great way to save for a rainy day.

The Influence of the Mega Church

The greater numbers of churches in America are in small towns and rural areas and have small membership, and therefore are subject to the self-appointed authority of individuals that most often use their position and some of the funds inappropriately. The self-appointment is based on the fact that a vast number of churches today basically are under the ownership or the strict guidance of the pastor. Small towns and rural communities depend heavily on churches for activities and pastors can be more significant and influential than the mayors.

Mega churches, minimum 2,000 in attendance on a weekly basis and the religious phenomenon of the 20th century, are not immune from being victimized by dishonest pastors. According to the website for the Hartford Institute for Religion Research, an estimated 5 million people in the U.S. attend over 1300 mega churches each week. I was a member of a pre-dominantly black mega church in Houston, Texas for 19 years. We, the members, showered the pastor with accolades, gifts, and financial support until he became a religious superstar. His lifestyle was lavish and he was not bashful in describing the things and events this lifestyle afforded. His oratorical, organizational, and management skills were overshadowed by his arrogance and lack of humility. These character flaws became more apparent as the membership increased. The church staff, deacon and trustee boards were comprised of business professionals and people with college degrees, and yet he was still allowed to practice inappropriate behavior. Notice the majority of the leaders of these mega churches in their multi-million dollar lifestyles enticing you with the subtle concept, "the more you give and increase your faith, the sooner you can live like me." According to the Prosperity Gospel, God wants everyone that has faith to live in abundance especially the charismatic pastor. These TV preachers, most are mega church pastors because small churches cannot afford the broadcast time, are redefining what it means to be a con artist.

A Christian church becomes a mega church by the acquisition of members from other churches. The growth is seldom attributed to new converts to Christianity. These are primarily members disgruntled enough to seek the confines of what they consider will be a better Christian church family. They are attracted to something different with better entertainment. A pastor is gratified when a new person is stirred emotionally and responds to a riveting sermon and the choir's music, lifeblood of the black church, by walking down the aisle to the front to express their desire to become a member. This is the high time of the worship service. There is very little interest in their reason for leaving the other church. I am amazed at the money spent by mega churches on advertising: newspaper, television, and billboards. Churches compete for members just as businesses compete for customers. No customers, no revenue. Imagine a sign on a building, "Church for Sale – Remaining Members Included." It is perplexing that God would allow a church to go out of business.

Today's mega churches are merely tax-exempt corporations under the stout management of Bible toting CEO's without the fear of being voted out by the board of directors. They are experts at mixing business with religion, identifying it as community development for the purpose of meeting the needs of the people. Their program ideas are very impressive from a business perspective. They are shrewd enough to place persons on the payroll that will adhere to their policies and will not challenge their authority. It is audacious of someone to challenge the authority of an individual called by God. I have experienced a pastor that hired individuals for full-time positions at the church with the stipulation that at least ten percent of their gross salary would be returned in the offering. In fact, my wife and I were chastised and asked by this same pastor to resign from a leadership position because we didn't follow this rule for giving even though we did not work at the church. The answer to your question is yes; we departed that church immediately. This pastor was starched in his rules because he was the founder and therefore it was his church. What would Jesus say concerning a pastor owning a church? I wonder what would Jesus say concerning pastors owning a Rolls Royce automobile, a jet plane, a helicopter to travel between churches in the same city, and a mansion on earth for a home? Carter G. Woodson, the father of the celebration of black history in the U.S., in his book *The Mis-Education of The Negro,* wrote the following:

> *"What the Negro church is, however, has been determined largely by what the white man has taught the race by precept and example. We must remember that the Negroes learned their religion from the early white Methodists and Baptists who evangelized the slaves and the poor whites when they were barred from proselytizing the aristocracy. The American white people themselves taught Negroes to specialize unduly in the "Praise the Lord," "Hallelujah" wor-*

*ship.... In the church where we have much free-
dom and independence we must get rid of
preachers who are not prepared to help the people they exploit. The public must refuse to support men of this type. Ministers who are the
creations of the old educational system must be
awakened, and if this is impossible they must be
dethroned. Those who keep the people in igno-
rance and play upon their emotions must be
exiled. The people have never been taught what
religion is, for most of the preachers find it eas-
ier to stimulate the superstition, which develops
in the unenlightened mind. Religion in such
hands, then, becomes something with which you
take advantage of weak people. Why try to
enlighten the people in such matters when
superstition serves just as well for exploitation?"*

With religion, we have too much emotion and very little
knowledge to support the conviction. A preacher stimulates
the congregant's emotions with an overwhelming flair for
obtaining wealth. Acquiring wealth is relatively simple when
you can convince enough people to give you a portion of
theirs on a regular basis. Blacks in America are victims of
deceit all too often and the black mega churches are doing it
expeditiously.

The mega church is like the new kid on the block with
all the latest high tech toys. It is very easy to make new
friends by offering to share your new fancy stuff. They will be
even closer friends if you promise to tell them how to get

those toys too. Imagine our community if 2,000 black people in various locations throughout the country were learning the truth on a weekly basis instead of being filled with "the holy ghost."

Missing the Mark

Promoting physical wellness is another area where the black church fails. Blacks in the United States encounter a disproportionate share of illness, disease, injury, disability, and death. Cancer and diabetes excel in the black community. We need messages necessary to guide people into behaviors that will prevent illness and disease that leads to injury, disability, and death. The key word is prevent. In order to prevent anything, we must know how it is defined and its causes. Termination of a human's life should only occur through an accident or the body's natural deterioration. We need truth not commercials and information that are disguised to enhance the sick-care industry. The sick-care industry, better known as healthcare, comprised of doctors, nurses, and hospitals that use pharmaceuticals for treatment, is contrast to holistic wellness. Is chemotherapy and radiation the best treatment for cancer? The quality of a human life should not be sacrificed to sustain private profit seeking enterprises. Pastors are in a quagmire regarding certain messages. They are unlikely to preach a true wellness message that disturbs the financial status of a member that happens to be a medical doctor that gives according to their riches. The high financial contributors to the church are well known by the pastors. Being trained for physical wellness is worth going to the same place, every week, to hear the same message from the same person. The church is certainly not the place for mental and emotional wellness. I conclude that Christians will never be receptive to these messages as long as they are mentally conditioned to attest all of life's events to either God or Satan. God receives praise for the good and Satan is blamed for the bad. What is the best solution for heart disease, the reduced consumption of fried chicken, prayer meetings, or the healing waters of Lourdes, France?

With the number of churches in the black communities, there should be a declining number of dishearten people struggling to survive. Conditions that cause despair in peoples' lives should be constantly decreasing. The black churches should represent all that is good for the people that provide its means for existence. Despite the little or no return on investment, there is plenty of high valued entertainment and fellowship: musicals, choir competitions, banquets, cookouts, concerts, and fashion shows. Black churches are a constant source for comedians' material and Hollywood movie scripts. It is very seldom that a white church and its pastor are mocked in a movie or television program. A singer that has little success in one genre of music can always try gospel. If you know someone in need of a helping hand it would be right as a fellow human to offer some assistance. You do not need the church to assist people in need. Someone once said that lighthouses are more helpful than churches.

Self - Discrimination

United we stand divided we fall is a battle cry for groups fighting for justice and civil rights. This fight appears to be permanently woven into the fabric of Black America;

however, divisiveness prevails in the black community when it comes to religion and the beliefs founded in the various Christian denominations. I cannot picture the occasion when a Baptist would extend a loving invitation to share conversation over a meal to a Jehovah's Witness. A Jehovah's Witness cannot attend a funeral service of a family member if it is conducted inside the church of any other denomination. That reminds me of the "whites/colored" signs back in Alabama. For many years, my parents went in different directions on Sunday morning; father a Methodist and mother a Baptist. I wonder what affects that had on their relationship. They are no longer here for me to ask. My sisters and I had to choose. Where would I find the truth? I remember my father having many discussions with other Baptists concerning baptism, sprinkling vs. submersion. Eventually, after the kids moved out, mom decided to join dad at the Christian Methodist Episcopal Church. From a religious perspective, the commonalities of these denominations in their beliefs do not overshadow the differences.

Reason for Segregation

The Bible breeds this attitude toward separation even in the family. The book of Matthew in Chapter 10 records Jesus as stating his purpose was not to bring peace but a sword, and to set a man against his father, a daughter against her mother, and a daughter-in-law against her mother-in-law. In 2 Corinthians Chapter 6, Paul encourages believers to be separate from unbelievers. I am considered an unbeliever or a heathen by definition and now my family and friends must decide whether to make me an outcast. A black atheist does not have a chance. These messages are very disturbing and when taken literally, provokes harmful prejudices and prevents like- mindedness in preparation in the battle for justice and correctness. In today's society, can black people afford to continue practicing this form of segregation?

Black Men and the Church

Regarding divisiveness, where are the black men on Sunday mornings? As stated, blacks attend church regularly and yet black families are constantly in peril. Couples attempt to maintain relationships in the mist of mental confusion. I think women are the most challenged because of society's demand for them to be strong and independent in contrast with the Bible teachings of being submissive and silent. Black churches are supported primarily by a majority of black women, and the pastors cater to this dichotomy. Their sermons are more apt to promote the virtues of women and announce the failures of men. Yet, there have been many instances of pastors taking sexual advantage of vulnerable women in the mist of a troubled marriage. Some do not need the excuse of a troubled marriage. On the following Sunday, he is in the pulpit preaching about infidelity and resisting the temptation of Satan. Pastors and religious impersonators thrive on the emotions of women and the needs of the ones that are single parents. Marriages fail regularly in America notwithstanding the Christian influence and so-called God's endorsement. Christianity lacks qualifications to define and offer practical guidelines for marriage otherwise we would not have pastors having experienced multiple divorces. A marriage is simply a partnership. The individuals, heterosexual or homosexual, decide the purpose, the rules, the time of commencement, and the time to separate.

I propose many black men recognize "the game" played by the preachers and choose to limit their participation, but are uncertain in their ability to express their reasons in addition to being in fear of losing their salvation. Lack of knowledge about Christianity and the conditioning regarding its necessity make it impossible to communicate the concerns. I must mention that of the black men that actively participate, too many are pawns adhering to the instructions of the master pastor. As a deacon, I saw how submissive men could be to the pastor. Religion is accepted as vital in our society and a black man that rejects this institution will be unsuitable for marriage particularly if they do not meet the financial requirements as in having a good job. If they make enough money, the absence of religion may be overlooked. Some black men choose not to attend church but choose not to discuss why, at least openly. We as black men in America are the preferred target for misguidance and displacement, which leaves the black family under the contrived security of institutions. Try this as an alternative, "a family that learns the truth together stays together."

Teaching the Children and Freedom of Choice

What about the children? I cannot fathom the neglect and abuse of a child. Our daughter attended a Christian private school for pre-kindergarten through eighth grade. Grades ninth through twelfth she attended a public school. She graduated from college in December 2008. We were committed to providing her a quality educational foundation in preparation for college and we also desired for her to become a quality person. My wife and I were fortunate enough to afford this type of environment. Because of our Christian beliefs, we felt that this particular school was suitable even though it was guided by a church denomination different from the Baptist church we attended and supported. It met our expectations. It provided the educational training and enhanced her religious growth. But she was not taught to be a critical thinker so we had to present that training even with our limited parenting skills. We encouraged her to ask questions. She was being conditioned to follow the normal path to success established by our society in addition to embracing religion.

The environment at this Christian school was not as conducive for the nurturing of black boys. Later we discovered that black boys, consistently, were treated astoundingly negatively. They were more readily recommended for the drug Ritalin and their opportunities for self-expression were stifled. The treatment was different if they displayed the athletic ability that could be utilized to sustain the school's basketball prominence.

Parents labeling their children with a religion are in contrast to how amicable parents are to allowing their children to choose for themselves their political affiliation. Who refers to a child at the age of ten as a democrat? At what age should a child be exposed to the brutalities, contradictions, and vagueness of the Bible? At what age is a child capable of comprehending the creation story, a talking snake, and the born in sin message? The rigorous Bible training my daughter received at the Christian school initiated questions that my wife and I were incapable of providing answers and neither were the school's teachers or the church's Bible scholars. She received typical explanations such as just believe and have faith. I am certain she remained confused for a long time. A confused child is an unhealthy child. I am trying to imagine our world when our children are encouraged to explore various and possible dissenting thoughts at an early age without fear of being ostracized. After a time period for a black Christian child to study the Bible, which should not take a lifetime, their next book for study should be Thomas Paine's *Age of Reason*. The third book on their reading list should be *The Mis-Education of The Negro* by Carter G. Woodson.

As parents and educators, including home schools, our responsibility should be to guide the children into knowledge and truth without the influence of shame and guilt. The best example of this is sex, and because of religion, it is poorly taught. I mention home schools because of their steady growth as a means to circumvent the public school system and surveys indicate the primary reason parents commit to home schooling is religious instructions. Christianity has taken sex, human's gift from nature, and made it a ball of confusion. Christianity tries to designate this incredible human response into the institution of marriage, which it has failed in defining. With the trauma of slavery and the dominance of Christianity, a black child in America is helpless and forced to seek solutions that could cause more devastation. Michael Eric Dyson, an ordained Baptist minister and a Princeton Ph. D., in his book, *Race Rules – Navigating the Color Line*, makes an admirable observation:

> *"Sex, after all, is a difficult subject to treat in the black church, or, for that matter, in any church. This*

is indeed ironic. After all, the Christian faith is grounded in the Incarnation, the belief that God took on flesh to redeem human beings, that belief is constantly trumped by Christianity's quarrels with the body. Its needs. Its desires. Its sheer materiality. But especially its sexual identity....In the main, a theology of eroticism must be developed to free black Christian sexuality from guilty repression or gutless promiscuity. Sermon after sermon counsels black Christians to abstain from loose behavior. To sleep only with our mates. To save sex for permanent love. And to defer sexual gratification until we are married. In black churches, as with most religious institutions, hardly anyone waits for marriage to have sex. People sleep with their neighbor's spouse. Casual sex is more than casually pursued. And because the needs of their bodies make them liars with bad consciences, some drown their demons in a sea of serial monogamies. Little of this is highly pleasurable, but it's pleasurable enough to make us unhappy. Ugh!"

Our youth today are strongly criticized for their lack of morals. The morality issue is not questioned when the Old Testament stories of Abraham's sexual encounter with Hagar, his wife's Egyptian maid, and Solomon's abundance of wives and concubines are examined. What lessons should our children learn from these stories? I must presume that Abraham's act predates adultery as sinful and therefore escapes condemnation since the Ten Commandments had not been written.

Children are taught at a very early age to revere pastors and church leaders while priests are secretly molesting some of their friends. Imagine that scar. Should religious institutions be convicted of child abuse? Is religion a contributor to mental illness in our children? I'll leave those questions for the experts to answer. Maybe the Catholic Church is doing us a favor by preventing their leaders from the responsibility of parenting. Now I have clarity in my sympathy for children of preachers.

Let's consider the ramifications if parents allowed their children, absent the fear of punishment, the freedom of choice; religion or no religion. If they choose religion, the type would be based on what's suitable for them, not family tradition. Now that would be freedom of or from religion. Tradition has nothing to do with the evolution of music, fashions, and new technology that attracts the attention of our children away from religious customs. Hip-Hop, Rap, sagging pants, and tattoos are compelling challenges for the old school church. There are some churches that continue to specify that women should not wear pants to church services and meetings. How's that for old time religion? If we are to teach our children about religion, make available to them the origin, doctrines, and historical development of all religions so they can make reasonable unbiased comparisons.

> *For these are all our children,*
> *We will profit by, or pay for,*
> *Whatever they become.*
>
> *- James Baldwin*

Continuation of Illusion

The condition of blacks in America can simply be described as being physically free but mentally enslaved. This only makes true freedom an illusion. Institutions, such as our government, monetary system, and religion, create these illusions, and it is very difficult to distinguish their identities. Each is camouflaged with the others whenever it is convenient; in God we trust stamped on the currency, politicians visiting the churches during a campaign, church worship services resembling a rock concert, laws to prevent same sex marriage, prayer at Wall Street and the twelve Federal Reserve Banks. It is significant when our presidents do not recognize the relevance of the separation of church and state. George W. Bush created the Faith Base Initiative and President Obama, obligated or not, chose to maintain this monetary breadbasket. President Obama is so engulfed in his Christian faith he needs five men as his spiritual advisors. Three are black and one of them served in this capacity for the previous president. Rest assured that their organizations are reaping financial benefits. My hope was for Barack Obama to be an instrument to remove black people's illusions but instead, as of this writing, he is a contributor. If you are curious, the constitution does allow for a non-religious person to be elected to an office in our government. Only a few years ago, per my estimation, religion would have been the last institution convicted for deceiving black people. Now it should be the first.

As a summary regarding the negative affects of church and religion, I will use the writing of W.E.B. DuBois in his final autobiography:

"At 17 I was in a missionary college where religious orthodoxy was stressed; but I was more developed to meet it with argument, which I did. My "morals" were sound, even a bit puritanic, but when a hidebound old deacon inveighed against dancing I rebelled. By the time of graduation I was still a 'believer' in orthodox religion, but had strong questions which were encouraged at Harvard. In Germany I became a freethinker and when I came to teach at an orthodox Methodist Negro school I was soon regarded with suspicion, especially when I refused to lead the students in public prayer. When I became head of a department at Atlanta, the engagement was held up because again I balked at leading in prayer, . . . I flatly refused again to join any church or sign any church creed. From my 30th year on I have increasingly regarded the church as an institution which defended such evils as slavery, color caste, exploitation of labor and war. I think the greatest gift of the Soviet Union to modern civilization was the dethronement of the clergy and the refusal to let religion be taught in the public schools."

CLOSING THOUGHTS

"Religion is the bane of the human mind."
-Dr. Henry Jones,
M.D. & Psychiatrist

Without the harmful restrictions of religion while having genuine respect and appreciation for the natural order of life, a person is free to observe issues that affect that order, and find solutions that will benefit all participants in the universe. No human or institution created by humans has the right to control and manipulate the thoughts and well being of other humans or any other living species in our universe. Freedom of thought and the ability to reason are human's most prized possessions. Religions destroy these aptitudes. Religion promotes prejudices, hatred, and confusion that could lead to mental illness. A person who hears voices telling them what to do is often considered schizophrenic. In our legal system, when a person commits a murder and uses the premise that God told them to do it, that person is classified as insane. A person who believes they are constantly being watched has paranoia. Does your pastor tell you God told him to do something or reminds you that God is watching? Is God watching and controlling the lives of all humans in the universe even the ones that think he does not exist? If God is love and omni-caring and meets your needs according to his timing, why bother God with prayer? Is there any proof of prayers being answered on behalf of the nation since the adoption of National Prayer Day in 1952? I guess God allowed catastrophes such as the 1989 earthquake in San Francisco, 911, and hurricane Katrina. Does your pastor tell you what God thinks about homosexuals or does he quote the writings of Paul, the self-appointed apostle and founder of Christianity? Is God acceptable to racism or is that the work of the devil? Did God make George W. Bush president? Did President Bush pray for God's guidance when he was authorizing the raining of bombs on the innocent people of Iraq, including children? Instead of encouraging the ability to gather truth on your own, religions tell you what to believe in order to mold your worldview.

In church there is a saying, "pray like it depends on God but work like it depends on you." If there is productivity from this approach, how can a reasonable intelligent person determine if God made the difference or his or her own effort? Self-reliance is the ability to depend on one's own efforts and judgments for sustenance. Self-reliance is a human instinct. Christians that are in need of a job, try this for a test. Pray vehemently to God for a job. Then do not send out any resumes, complete any job applications, place any phone calls, or send any emails. Remain patiently at home and prepare for your start date on your new job. You may learn the true value of prayer. As a reminder, the Bible records Jesus instructing you to pray in your closet. My disinterest in religious type prayer does not mean I do not encourage moments of meditation, adequate time for self-evaluation, and maintaining an attitude of appreciation. These are aspects associated with spirituality, which I view completely different from religion. Spirituality is defined, guided, and practiced solely by the individual. Prayer dependency and self-reliance cannot coexist.

Considering all religions, especially Christianity, and their various denominations, which one is the truth? Of the three main branches of Christianity, Catholic, Orthodox, and Protestant, which one has the inside track to heaven? Each religion inherently, based on their own book, has to promote itself as being the "right" religion, which in turn deems the other religions as "wrong." This is an uncompromising duality. For Christians, the Bible contains numerous contradictions. Contradictions give birth to false teachings and confusion. Confusion hinders the ability to make decisions, which gives birth to frustration that can manifest harmful decisions. I do not think a God that created such a magnificent universe would give us a book like the Bible or any of these so called holy books.

Christianity, the world's largest religion with an estimated 2.1 billion adherents comprising around 34,000 separate denominations including the ones identified as non-denominational, has distorted the concept of moral judgment by infusing concepts such as sin. For example, the abortion issue is a religious debate. The loudest mouthpiece against it, promoting pro-life, are those religions that are not oppose to war. The Middle East is a religious mess. Our government, which is under the operation of highly religious people, dropped two atomic bombs that killed an estimated 210,000 people and takes pride in its military. The Bible gives us a story about how God got angry with King Saul because Saul did not completely destroy a nation, including children, as instructed by God (1 Samuel 15). Why abortion is wrong but war is right? Christians in the military seem to me to be anti-Jesus' teachings. Jesus supposedly infers the idea of turning the other cheek. Is our military personnel warriors for God and should they carry a gun in one hand and a Bible in the other? New Testament Bible based Christians should not be adamant in their search for Osama (Where in the World Is) Bin Laden to avenge the events of 911. They should be merciful and forgiving, but more importantly determined to know the truth of all persons minutely responsible for this massacre. Why abortion is wrong, but pharmaceuticals, toxic chemicals, and alcohol that are harmful and often kill are okay? Alcohol contributes to more than 100,000 deaths in the U.S. alone. Alcohol has its way of relieving people of their inhibitions that contribute to more sexual activity and unplanned pregnancies. I have yet to see a report of a group of evangelicals protesting in front of a liquor store demanding its closing. If having an abortion is a crime, what should be the punishment? Should the doctor be executed by a Christian "hit-man" or given life in prison? Christianity is incapable of determining and influencing morality for all humans.

Why, in the very religious United States, is the crime rate so high? The U.S. has the highest incarceration rate, 762 per 100,000 residents, of all other nations. Our justice system, injustice by its practice, is in peril because the officials, judges, attorneys, and police, are victims of this capitalistic society as often as the individuals they attempt to punish or defend. Our society is morally bankrupt primarily because of the confusion ingested by religious dogma. Compared to Christians, the number of agnostics or atheists in our prison system is low. It is terrifying to think of 2.1 billion people trying to convert all other humans to their system of beliefs and distorted views, and defining what is right and wrong.

Regarding our prison system, a black Christian church that sponsors a prison ministry but is not stern in their efforts to promote justice and correctness at the courthouse is shameful. Blacks comprise 46% of the prison population. Contrary to its appearance, the purpose of the ministry is to proselytize and grow the membership. It does not prevent blacks, especially black men, from false imprisonment even with Christians as judges and in the jury box. Religion in the prisons is a façade for big business and funds for non-profit organizations. Guiding the inmates to conversion, becoming born again believers, does not guarantee a job opportunity when they are released.

Same sex marriage is another issue at the forefront of political debate masked as a moral threat to society. Aside from the jurisdiction of religions, the only human social order that the relationship between a man and a woman can dictate is reproduction. Everything else is a matter of individual choices and subject to being redefined. Marriage and family are at this crossroad because of homosexuality. We must try to understand its cause, assuming it is not natural, determine whether it proposes imminent danger to human existence, and then seek evaluations and conclusions through science. We cannot afford this responsibility to be managed under the deluded beliefs of religions, especially Christian Fundamentalist. Are Christians ready to administer punishment for all homosexuals in addition to the upcoming judgment day? From my perspective, homosexuals should take a stand against religions and their prejudices. If they have the courage to pronounce their plight as an unavoidable condition, that same courage can be used to avoid the untruth and deceit of religions. Homosexual and non-religious should be synonymous. In contrast, there are some people that are concern about birth rates and over population which homosexuality is a solution to both. I consider racism, HIV/AIDS, cancer, poverty, war promotion, and the Federal Reserve System as true threats that demand immediate solutions in lieu of wasting time on trivial issues.

Our universe is in need of new ideas, rational thought, and human behavior that will sustain its existence. Our universe does not need more entrepreneurs, millionaires, or capitalists filled with greed hiding behind religion. More importantly, we cannot tolerate any more religious politicians. Politicians are not trained to solve problems. They are only capable of making laws that are polluted by religion and meet the approval of religious zealots and highly financed lobbyists. Religions have caused too much destruction and the delusion of truth. Religion allows the mysterious to override facts and the supernatural to be more relevant than the natural.

Today, I relish the opportunity to challenge black Americans and their need for religion, especially Christianity. Consider this as freedom from bondage of another institution. My quest is to share my discovery of this freedom and how I allowed my thoughts to be guided toward refreshing ideals by reading and listening to the thoughts expressed by other people, particularly when those thoughts promote the betterment of humankind. I was unafraid to examine and ask questions. I prefer to have facts rather than belief. Some define belief as an assumed truth. I define belief as an opinion without facts that subsequently influences behavior. Our society compels us to refrain from challenging any statement preceded by the words "I believe." Try using "I think" instead.

With adequate information, humans have the ability to make rational and logical decisions, to select from choices. I chose to change something significant in my life because it just made sense. I no longer subscribe to the reward of heaven and the punishment of hell because I do not have evidence that support their existence. I do not assumed them to be true. A book with unknown writers that is tainted with contradictions cannot be credible evidence. The reality of an afterlife no longer harbors in my consciousness, but I will gladly reconsider when enough facts are presented. We should treasure and protect freedom to think. This quest is to enlighten by stirring the mixture of cogent thoughts.

In spite of our history and how we are constantly reminded of its role, I ponder the existence of blacks in the United States free from religion. What a travesty if it is necessary to attend a service every week, with cash, check, or debit card in hand, to hear the same person, teach the same message, using the same book, adhering to blind faith. Blacks choosing to attend pre-dominantly white churches is not an alternative. A white pastor is not better than a black pastor. What a travesty to be obligated to an institution and its practices primarily because of tradition and respect for family. I refuse to entertain the thought that black people in America lack the ability to utilize reason and logic. Will we always be in need of a Moses, or a savior? Should we continue to impose conditions from slavery, fear and confusion, on our children or should those negatives be replaced by the skill of thinking? Let's encourage and equip them to decipher truth from mystery in all things, including the Bible. Fear is life's holding cell. The acquisition of knowledge and truth are the only means for escape.

Black Americans must embrace solutions and the courage to end victimization by institutions that stimulate society's ills while offering a false sense of security. Considering that society has given ample time, I do not think religion, especially Christianity, will ever provide tangible solutions for racism, poverty, crime, and a poor educational system. Humans that are fortunate to be without any physical or learning disabilities should not seek security in other humans or institutions, especially religions.

In the words of Thomas Paine written in his pamphlet the *Common Sense:*

> *"To conclude, however strange it may appear to some, or however unwilling they may be to think so, matters not, but many strong and striking reasons may be given, to show, that nothing can settle our affairs so expeditiously as an open and determined declaration for independence."*

Our future can be brighter with the dark clouds of religions removed. We can be free mentally when the chains of religious dogma are broken. Religion to black Americans is analogous to Great Britain's former hold on the original 13 colonies and I declare independence.

Bible Contradictions

The following are a few of the many contradictions for your Bible study:

How many pairs of animals did God tell Noah to take into the ark?
- Two – Genesis 6:19,20
- Seven – Genesis 7:2

Who appeared to Moses in the burning bush?
- God – Exodus 3:4; Mark 12:26
- Angel – Exodus 3:2; Acts 7:35

Did Joshua and the Israelites capture Jerusalem?
- Yes – Joshua 10:23,40
- No – Joshua 15:63

Does God repent?
- No – Numbers 3:16; 1 Samuel 15:29; Ezekiel 24:14; Malachi 3:6
- Yes – Genesis 6:6; Exodus 32:14; Deuteronomy 32:36; 1 Samuel 15:11; Jeremiah 18:8

Is it ok to call someone a fool?
- No – Matthew 5:22
- Yes – Matthew 23:17; Luke 11:40, 24:25; 1 Corinthians 15:36

What will happen to Jews when they die?
- They will be saved – Romans 11:26
- They will go to hell – Mat 8:12

Will the earth last forever?
- Yes – Deuteronomy 4:40; Psalms 37:29,78:69; Ecclesiastes 1:4
- No – Psalms 102:25-26; Isaiah 65:17; Matthew 24:35; 2 Peter 3:10

How long does God's anger last?
- Moment – Psalms 30:5; Jeremiah 3:12; Micah 7:18
- Long Time – Numbers 32:13; Jeremiah 17:4

Should Christians pray in public?
- No – Matthew 6:5-6
- Yes – 1 Timothy 2:8

Did Jesus bear his own cross?
- No – Matthew 27:31-32
- Yes – John 19:17

When (at what time of day) was Jesus crucified?
- At the 3rd hour – Mark 15:25
- After the 6th hour – John 19:14-16

What color was Jesus' robe?
- Scarlet – Matthew 27:28
- Purple – Mark 15:17; John 19:2

What was the exact wording on Jesus' cross?
- This is Jesus the King of the Jews – Matthew 27:37
- The King of the Jews – Mark 15:26
- This is the King of the Jews – Luke 23:38
- Jesus of Nazareth, the King of the Jews – John 19:19

Apart from Jesus did anyone else ascend to heaven?
- No – John 3:13
- Yes – 2 Kings 2:11

Reference Bibliography

Douglas, Frederick. *Narrative of the Life of Frederick Douglas*. Dover Publications, New York, NY.

DuBois, W.E.B. *The Autobiography of W.E.B. DuBois – A Soliloquy on Viewing My Life from the Last Decade of Its First Century*. International Publishers

Dyson, Michael Eric. *Race Rules – Navigating the Color Line*. First Vintage Books Edition.

Glaude, Eddie S. and West, Cornell. *African American Religious Thought: An Anthology*. Westminister John Knox Press.

Leary, Joy Degruy. *Post Traumatic Slave Syndrome: America's Legacy of Enduring Injury and Healing*. Uptone Press, Milwaukie, Oregon.

Library of America. *Thomas Paine – Collected Writings (Age of Reason, Common Sense)*.

The Lockman Foundation. *New American Standard Bible.* Foundation Publications, Anaheim, CA.

Woodson, Carter G. *The Mis-Education of the Negro.* Classic House Books, New York, NY.

Website: www.mrlincolnandfreedom.org. *The Lincoln-Douglas Debates.*

Website: www.infidels.org/library/historical/robert_ingersoll/ what_is_religion.html. *Robert G. Ingersoll - What is Religion?*

Website: www.infidels.org/library/historical/ robert_ingersoll/. *Robert G. Ingersoll - An Address to Colored People.*

Suggested Reading List

Books

The Autobiography of W.E.B. DuBois – A Soliloquy on Viewing My Life from the Last Decade of Its First Century – W.E.B. DuBois

Post Traumatic Slave Syndrome: America's Legacy of Enduring Injury and Healing. – Joy Degruy Leary

Letter To a Christian Nation – Sam Harris

Thomas Paine – Collected Writings (Age of Reason, Common Sense) – Library of America

Narrative of the Life of Frederick Douglas - Frederick Douglas

The Mis-Education of the Negro – Carter G. Woodson

God Delusion – Richard Dawkins

History of God – Karen Armstrong

Jesus Words Only – Douglas J. Del Tondo

The Kingdom That Turned the World Upside Down – David W. Bercot

The Mythmaker: Paul and the Inventions of Christianity – Hyam Maccoby

Conversations with God; an uncommon dialogue – Neale Donald Walsh

The Black Humanist Experience: An Alternative to Religion – Norm R. Allen, Jr., Editor

Websites

www.religoustolerance.org

www.infidels.org/library/historical/robert_ingersoll.html

http://philosopedia.org/index.php/Category:African_American_Freethinkers

www.ffrf.org Freedom from Religion Foundation

http://www.users.drew.edu/%7Ejlenz/brs.html Bertrand Russell Society

LaVergne, TN USA
30 December 2009
168540LV00002B/3/P